Edward Wynkoop
Soldier and Indian Agent

Edward Wynkoop
Soldier and Indian Agent

NOW YOU KNOW BIOS

Number Seventeen in the Series

Nancy Oswald

Filter Press, LLC
Palmer Lake, Colorado

In memory of my grandmother, Mabel DeBont,
biography lover, history lover,
storyteller, and reader.

ISBN: 978-0-86541-184-5
Library of Congress Control Number: 2014938519

Cover image courtesy Denver Public Library, Western History Collection, X-22195
George D. Wakely, photographer. Used with permission.

Copyright ©2014 Nancy Oswald. All rights reserved.

No part of this book may be reproduced or transmitted in any form or by any means, electronic or mechanical, by sound recording or by any information storage and retrieval system, without permission in writing from the publisher.
Email inquiries to info@FilterPressBooks.com.

Printed in United States of America

Contents

1. Young Ned 1
2. The Pull of the West 4
3. Early Days in Denver 9
4. Civil War Soldier 14
5. A Clash of Cultures 21
6. The Tall Chief 27
7. Bloody Sand Creek 35
8. Wynkoop Speaks Out 40
9. Working for Peace 43
10. Indian Agent 48
11. Wynkoop's Lasting Legacy 54

Timeline 57
Glossary 61
Bibliography 64
Index 67
Acknowledgments 69
About the Author 70

Edward Wanshaer Wynkoop, 1836-1891

1 Young Ned

When Edward W. Wynkoop was a child, he had no way of knowing that one day he would earn the respect of the famous Cheyenne chief, Black Kettle. He did not know he would ride into a camp of more than one thousand Cheyenne warriors or that he would become a defender of the **Plains Indians**. Young Edward could not predict these things. In fact, when he was born, few Americans had traveled west of the Mississippi River. By the time he died, the United States had grown from twenty-five to forty-four states.

Edward was born June 19, 1836, in Philadelphia, Pennsylvania. A year later, his father died. His mother was left to raise their seven children: Frank, Anna, Emily, John, Charles, George, and Edward. Edward was the youngest. Edward was adored by the family,

◆

2 Edward Wynkoop

who nicknamed him Neddy. As he grew up, his friends called him Ned. Edward's siblings passed on to him their father's love of poetry and other arts, a sense of duty, and a love of country. He also learned the importance of hard work.

Edward's father had served in the **militia** during the War of 1812. Edward's brother Frank also served in the military. During the Mexican-American War, Frank noticed that the Irish soldiers were treated unfairly. When he returned home, he started a business that hired only Irish workers. Frank's decision was unpopular, but he thought it was the right thing to do. Frank's courage taught Edward the importance of standing up for his beliefs.

Through his family, Edward learned about the world beyond the city of Philadelphia. His brother Charlie became an actor and managed his own theater company presenting plays in the South and many other places. Edward's sister Emily was the first in the family to travel to the West. Her second husband, William Brindle, was a **surveyor** in the Kansas and Nebraska Territories.

At the time of the Brindles' move to Kansas, the country was deeply divided over whether **slavery** would be tolerated in any part of the United States. The laws at that time allowed the people in Kansas and Nebraska Territories to decide whether or not slavery would be allowed. Brindle was an **abolitionist** and wrote about his opinions in the newspaper. The people who wanted slavery did not like Brindle speaking out against it. By standing against slavery, Emily and her husband set another example in courage for Edward.

Edward grew up to be a handsome and confident young man. He was a good student, could speak and write well, and got along with other people. He also knew the difference between right and wrong.

2 The Pull of the West

Edward had an itch to do something exciting with his life. In 1856 he traveled to Lecompton, Kansas, to stay with Emily and work as a clerk in his brother-in-law's land office. William Brindle managed the sale of public lands in the territory.

Even though he worked as a clerk, Edward wore **buckskins** and carried a knife. He strapped on a revolver before he left the house. Violence in Kansas was a part of life and often exploded between those who wanted slavery and those who did not. Emily and her husband had muskets on every floor of their cabin, including the cellar. Being armed was common on the **frontier**. Dangers came in many forms.

When Brindle closed his land office business, Edward went with him to St. Louis, Missouri, to deliver a valuable shipment of gold. They met robbers on the trail and had to think fast to get away. They changed direction and made a daring escape by moonlight. This was the first time Edward was in a life-or-death situation, but it would not be the last.

Shortly after this trip, Edward met James W. Denver, the governor of Kansas Territory. Denver had met Edward's brother Frank during the Mexican-American War, and he took a liking to Edward. Governor Denver showed him a map of the Pikes Peak region where gold had been recently discovered. Edward was ready for a new adventure. In the fall of 1858, he joined a **land development company** heading west to the goldfields. Although he was new to the region, Edward was appointed sheriff for Arapahoe County, a huge area in the western part of Kansas Territory. Edward and sixteen companions set out by wagon train on the Santa Fe Trail planning to reach the goldfields via the southern route that skirted Pikes Peak.

As they traveled west, Edward had his first encounter with Native Americans. A group of Comanche and Kiowa Indians approached the wagon train and demanded the return of a mule that they claimed belonged to them. A man in Wynkoop's group had recently traded a horse for the mule, and he refused to give it back. The Indians followed the wagon train, repeating their request for the mule. One of the Indians challenged Edward to a horse race. During the race Edward's rifle bounced on his saddle and discharged. This upset the Indians, who threatened to attack. The wagons circled, but no more shots were fired. After a long, uneasy wait, the Indians rode away. If the Indians had been forced into a battle, the journey might have ended differently.

Many miles later Wynkoop and his group had the unforgettable experience of seeing the Rocky Mountains for the first time. It was a clear, frosty morning, and Wynkoop later wrote this description:

> Will anyone ever forget the first sight the Rocky Mountains. I never shall; it was the thirty-fifth day after leaving Topeka on a clear bright frosty morning, we had just come up onto a piece of table land when there was one simultaneous cheer which rang clear and hearty over those bleak plains, cheers from only seventeen throats, but such cheers, no seventeen men ever gave such cheers before; we almost imagined they were carried back over seven hundred miles of desert to the ears of our anxious friends, for

there before us, darting their snowcapped points into the blue outer were the three Spanish Peaks of the Rocky Mountains.

Later in the trip, Wynkoop and his party joined a land development company owned by William Larimer Jr., an early settler who helped found Denver City. On November 2, 1858, the group reached a settlement of a few rough buildings along the South Platte River and Cherry Creek. The trip had not been easy. During the last month, all of their horses and saddles were stolen, their supplies were low, and they had fought their way through twelve inches of snow.

Wynkoop's problems were not over. When he and Larimer arrived, much of the best land in the area had already been claimed by the St. Charles Town Company. Wynkoop told the settlers in the St. Charles Town Company that he and his company had been appointed by Governor Denver to take charge of the area. This did not go over well. The people with the St. Charles Company had already started building. They liked making their own rules and did not want outside government.

Know More!

New Towns in the West

Colorado was unsettled land when Wynkoop arrived. Towns were just getting started. Investors and settlers formed land companies to buy large tracts of land from the US government. The companies resold the land and made decisions about how the land would be used.

If you could create your own town and choose any name you wanted, what would it be? What problems and challenges would you face when starting a new town? With a partner, make a list of things you would need to do. Search the web for photos of old pioneer towns west of the Mississippi River. Use the photos for ideas and draw a picture of a pioneer town you would like to live in.

3 Denver City

Wynkoop and his party decided someone needed to return to Kansas to **incorporate** the Denver City Town Company. If not done right away, they might lose their chance to claim the land for themselves. It was already winter and the trip would be risky, but Wynkoop and Albert Steinberger volunteered to go.

The two men faced many hardships during the long trip along the northern route into Nebraska Territory. Temperatures dropped below freezing. The creeks and rivers were icy and crossing them was dangerous. Huddled together in a wagon pulled by two mules, they fought off the cold. Wynkoop nearly lost his feet to **frostbite**. Their wagon broke through the ice on the Platte River, killing one mule and sinking their supplies. They were robbed of their **provisions** by a group of

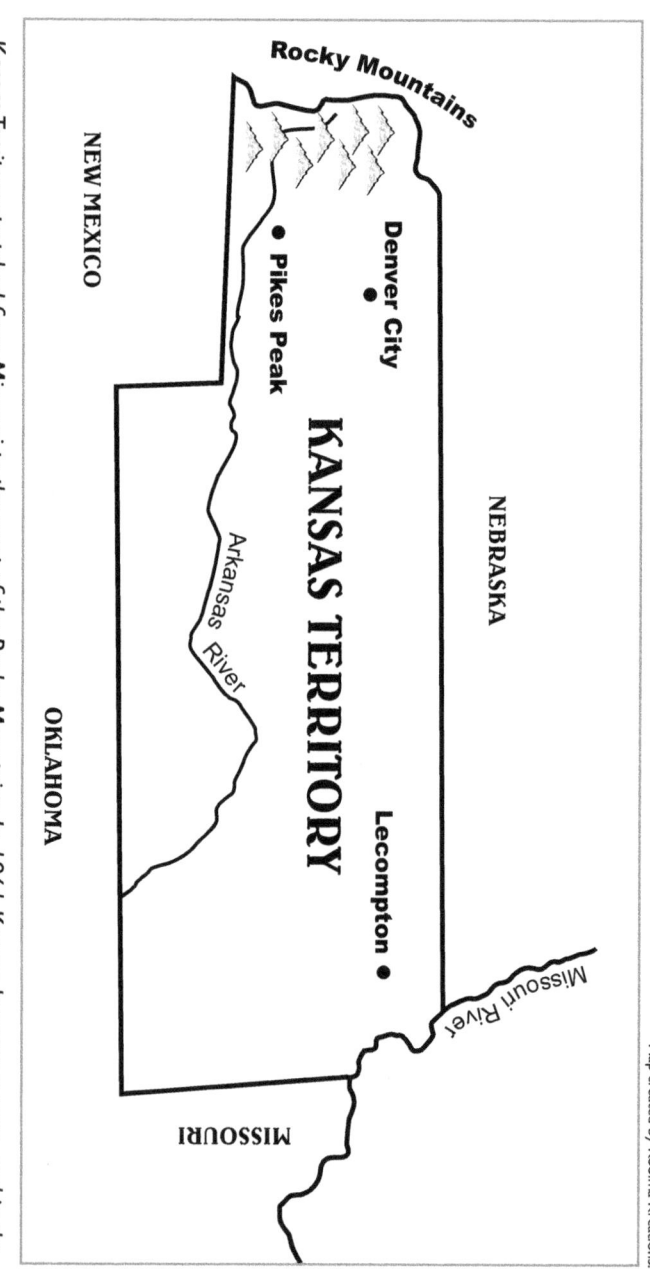

Kansas Territory stretched from Missouri to the crest of the Rocky Mountains. In 1861 Kansas became a state, and in the same year, citizens living in the western part of Kansas Territory voted to form a new territory called Colorado Territory.

Pawnee Indians. Along the way, they were helped by some white hunters and the Arapaho Indians. Tired, ragged, and weary, they arrived in Omaha on January 5, 1859. The journey from Denver City had taken a month.

In Omaha, people crowded around Wynkoop and Steinberger to ask about the goldfields. Their eyes lit up when Steinberger showed them a gold nugget. Everywhere they went, people wanted to know about the discovery of gold. They wondered if the chance to get rich would be worth the long journey.

Wynkoop shared his experiences with people, but he also had work to do. He continued to Lecompton, Kansas, where he intended to incorporate the Denver City Town Company. He was too late. St. Charles Town Company had already filed papers to incorporate Denver. After some discussion, Wynkoop convinced the St. Charles Town people that he and the other members of his group should be part of their company. He was eager to return to Arapahoe County, but he was not able to leave until September 5, 1859.

On their way back to the Pikes Peak region, they met familiar prospectors headed east. These men were poorer than when they began. Some blamed Wynkoop for their bad luck because it was on his word and information that they had made the long journey to look for gold. The men were so angry with Wynkoop that he sometimes feared for his life.

During the months Wynkoop had been away, the settlement along Cherry Creek had changed. The area was growing. Prospectors and settlers arrived daily. The people in the town needed food, clothing, shelter, and entertainment. A new type of traveler moved west to start businesses and provide services to the fast growing **population**.

When Edward and his party reached the new Denver City, a **boomtown** had replaced the handful of shacks that he had left behind. The town had meat shops, barber shops, grocery stores, gambling houses, restaurants, and a weekly newspaper—the *Rocky Mountain News*. In addition, the people living in the area had decided they wanted to separate from Kansas and form a new territory called Colorado Territory. Things were changing quickly.

Wynkoop still had his job as sheriff. The job did not pay well. To make extra money, he took a job acting at the theater in Apollo Hall. This made for some fun and excitement. Once, in 1861, he persuaded Chief Left

Hand to talk to the audience. Chief Left Hand told the audience that his people did not want to be their enemy. Apollo Hall is also where he met his future wife, Louise Wakely, a beautiful young actress.

As Wynkoop settled down in Denver City, the rest of the country was in turmoil. Abraham Lincoln had been elected the sixteenth president of the United States, and the country was on the verge of the American Civil War. In December 1860, the first Southern state **seceded** from the Union. The next year, Colorado became a territory independent of Kansas. The *Rocky Mountain News* changed to a daily paper, and Wynkoop was elected sheriff instead of being appointed. With his election came better pay.

Sheriff Wynkoop had many responsibilities. Denver was filled with **ruffians.** Wynkoop investigated murders, buried the victims, and calmed violent outbreaks and disagreements. He was good with a gun and not afraid to use it. Wynkoop was also outspoken. If he believed in something, he stood up for it. His views on slavery upset those who supported the South, but he did not waver from his abolitionist views.

4 Civil War Soldier

The United States was split between the Northern and Southern states over slavery. People in Colorado Territory had to decide where they stood on slavery. Angry and armed men from both sides filled the streets of Denver. The northern supporters outnumbered the southerners and drove Denver's first mayor out of town. When the Confederates, as the armies of the Southern states were called, threatened to invade Colorado Territory, Governor William Gilpin took action. To protect the goldfields, Gilpin organized the first two companies of volunteer soldiers. Wynkoop enlisted in Company A as a second lieutenant on July 31, 1861.

Also in 1861, Wynkoop quit his acting job and left his position as sheriff. He married Louise, and they celebrated the birth of their first son, Edward Estill.

Even though he had little military experience, he was soon promoted to captain. Military service would be a part of Wynkoop's life for many years to come.

Early in his military career, Wynkoop met John Chivington. Chivington, who stood six-feet seven-inches tall and weighed more than 250 pounds, had a forceful personality. He earned the name the "Fighting Parson" by preaching against slavery with two pistols crossed in front of him.

Wynkoop met Chivington at Camp Weld, a military outpost two miles north of Denver. At first, he liked him because they had many things in common. Both men were strong abolitionists and shared many of the same religious beliefs. Both were persuasive and charming, and neither would back down from a fight. Years later, disagreement over the treatment of the Plains Indians would end their friendship.

John Milton Chivington was a Methodist minister and soldier in the US Army.

For now Wynkoop and Chivington worked together to prepare for an invasion by the Confederates. Wynkoop was in charge of Company A. The officer above him was Major Chivington. Wynkoop and the other volunteer soldiers left Camp Weld on February 22, 1862, ready to defend the Colorado goldfields.

Confederate General Henry Sibley and his troops had set out for Colorado from Texas in October 1861. Sibley did not expect much of a fight from the Colorado Volunteers. His plan was to travel through New Mexico Territory and attack the Colorado goldfields from the south. He did not know that the volunteer Union soldiers had been preparing for the fight.

The volunteers traveled through deep snow and below-freezing temperatures toward New Mexico Territory. They reached the Purgatoire River where they met more volunteer troops. On March 7, they crossed Raton Pass. They were tired, weary, and wet. It took more than two weeks to follow the Red River to the Rio Grande. From there they traveled to Glorieta Pass, a day's march from Santa Fe.

On March 26, Wynkoop and his men met around 300 Confederate soldiers near Apache Canyon. Wynkoop's company and Company E were assigned to

skirmish while Company D got into a better fighting position. The soldiers cleared the hillside allowing Company D to circle around for an attack. Company D attacked, and the Confederates retreated.

Two days later, a second battle took place in Apache Canyon. By this time, the Confederate force had grown to more than 1,200 men, and the Union side had added 900 men. The battle lasted throughout the day. By evening the Union commander, Colonel John Slough, asked for a **truce,** and his men retreated.

While Slough and his men were fighting, Chivington's troops, including Wynkoop's Company A, climbed a steep **mesa** that overlooked the Confederate supply camp. Wynkoop's troops scrambled to the top of the mesa then slid down a treacherous slope into the supply camp and overpowered the guards. Company A destroyed the Confederates' wagons and supplies. Without supplies the Confederates were forced to retreat to Santa Fe and from there, make the long march back to Texas.

After the Battle of Glorieta Pass, Wynkoop was promoted to the rank of major. Chivington was promoted to colonel. It took until April 1862 for the Colorado Volunteers to completely sweep the

Confederates from New Mexico Territory. Company A remained in New Mexico to protect against future threats from the south. Wynkoop was put in charge of Fort Craig, located 130 miles south of Santa Fe, to watch for another Confederate invasion.

Wynkoop liked being in charge of the fort but missed his wife. He asked Louise to bring their little boy and come live at the fort. He also allowed the other men to bring their families. This did not normally happen on isolated posts, but it made the men happier and relieved the boredom of fort life. During Wynkoop's military career, Louise divided her time between living alone with their children and joining her husband wherever he was assigned.

In January 1863, Wynkoop returned to Camp Weld. In February he received an award for his leadership and courage in the Battle of Glorieta Pass. At the award ceremony he said that, if needed, he would give his life for the Union cause. That same month, Louise gave birth to a daughter they named Emily. There was much to celebrate, and wherever Wynkoop went, people admired and looked up to him.

While serving his country, Wynkoop came close to death many times. However, during the next part of

Louise Wakely married Major Wynkoop in 1861. She and their children often moved to the remote forts where Wynkoop was assigned.

his life, his fame would fade. Wynkoop was often in situations where he had to stand up for what he believed was right instead of taking an easier and more popular path. His values would be put to a strong test.

5 A Clash of Cultures

In Colorado Territory, settlements spread. Denver's population had grown to more than 4,000 people by 1863. Gold was discovered in the foothills of the Rockies, and towns such as Central City sprang up. Arapahoe County, which had been an area where Indians and early fur traders met to trade, changed rapidly. The houses of white settlers began to replace the tepees of the Arapaho and other Indian tribes. The peaceful relations between the settlers and Native Americans disappeared.

The Colorado Volunteers had a new job. Instead of fighting Confederate soldiers, they tried to keep the peace between **homesteaders** and the Indians. Under the leadership of Colonel Chivington, the military turned its attention to the Indians of the Plains.

Wynkoop became an Indian fighter. His first assignment was to find and punish a group of Ute warriors who had been raiding and stealing stock from settlers. After days of tracking and backtracking the Utes, Wynkoop ended up back in Camp Weld. He had traveled the border between Colorado and Wyoming Territories and ridden miles through western Colorado without ever seeing an Indian.

Tensions between the white settlers and the Indians worsened. Attacks by the military on the Cheyenne and other Plains Indians increased. Lieutenant George Eayre responded to a report that Indians had stolen livestock near Big Sandy Creek. He set out from Camp Weld and burned two Cheyenne villages, both of them empty because the Indians had fled.

Among the settlers, fear of the Indians grew. The *Rocky Mountain News* wrote that everyone should "shoulder his gun" for protection. Another newspaper, the *Commonwealth,* disagreed and wrote that there was no reason for people to be frightened of the Indians.

Communication in the West was slow, and it was not always accurate. It took days for military reports to reach officers at forts. The details of an event between settlers and Indians were not known until long after it happened. Rumors turned into stories that were filled with untruths. The rumors and half-truths made things worse. Not knowing the truth, people let their imaginations run wild.

In the spring of 1864, when Wynkoop returned from a trip east to see his mother, all of Colorado Territory had turned into a boiling pot of mistrust between the whites and Indians. In May Wynkoop was assigned the command of Fort Lyon in southeastern Colorado. When he arrived, the fort was in poor condition. The

Know More!

Communication on the Frontier

The first telegraph lines were laid in Denver in 1863. Until then, news traveled only as fast as the fastest horse and rider could travel. Sometimes information was inaccurately reported. Play this game to see how easy it is to change a message.

Sit in a line with your classmates. The person at the front of the line whispers some news to the next person. The second person repeats the news to the next person in line. Continue repeating the news until the news reaches the end of the line. The person at the end of the line tells what he or she heard. Compare what was heard at the end of the line with what was said to begin the game.

scant food was poor quality, and the buildings needed repair. He set his men to work on repairs and tried to get better **rations** for them. Cheyenne Indians were camped nearby, and Wynkoop contacted Colonel Chivington for clear orders regarding the Indians.

On May 16, while Wynkoop was settling in at Fort Lyon, Lieutenant Eayre attacked the Cheyenne at their Ash Creek camp. When the Cheyenne saw Eayre's men coming, Chief Lean Bear rode down from the camp

Know More!

Presidential Peace Medals

Beginning with George Washington and continuing through Benjamin Harrison, US presidents gave peace medals to important Native American leaders. The medals were often given as a token of friendship to tribal chiefs when a treaty was signed. Lean Bear's Lincoln Peace Medal had an image of President Lincoln on one side and a scene of a settler plowing on the reverse. The reverse also showed a schoolhouse with children playing baseball in the school yard.

to talk with Eayre. Lean Bear wore the peace medal that President Abraham Lincoln had given him when he went to Washington, DC, on a peace mission. Before Lean Bear could speak, he and a younger chief were shot and killed. Seeing two of their leaders fall, the Cheyenne attacked. Black Kettle rode among the warriors shouting, "Do not make war." Black Kettle temporarily stopped the fight, and Eayre and his men retreated. If it had not been for Chief Black Kettle, many more soldiers would have died.

Wynkoop did not know Eayre's men had killed Lean Bear. He was at Fort Lyon doing his best to prepare the fort against all types of threats, including a rumor that the Confederates were returning. In addition, Wynkoop had received word from Chivington that any Indians found in the area of Fort Lyon should be killed. Wynkoop had only 129 officers and men at the fort. He asked for **reinforcements**, and in June, Captain Silas Soule arrived with his troops to assist Wynkoop. However, that still was not enough men to protect the entire southeastern corner of the territory.

After the attack at Ash Creek, angry Cheyenne warriors **retaliated** for the deaths of their chiefs. They raided homesteads and wagon trains along the Arkansas and Platte Rivers. The Cheyenne stopped supply trains and cut telegraph wires. The mail could not get through, and settlers felt unsafe traveling.

On June 27, 1864, Governor John Evans wrote a letter addressed "To the Friendly Indians of the Plains." In it he asked the Indians who were "not at war" to report to forts closest to them. In August, however, Evans sent out different information. He told the people of Colorado to take up arms and pursue "the hostile Indians of the Plains."

A Cheyenne chief named One-Eye did not know anything about Evans' second **proclamation.** He set off in early September to deliver two letters from Chief Black Kettle asking to make peace with the whites. The letters had been written by **interpreters**, and one of them was to be delivered to the person in charge of Fort Lyon.

Fort Lyon soldiers were still under orders from Chivington to kill Indians in the area. By luck, One-Eye was taken prisoner instead of killed. Major Wynkoop opened the letter. Black Kettle wanted to exchange white captives for the Indian prisoners that he thought were being held in Denver. He also wanted the whites to make peace with the Cheyenne, Arapaho, Kiowa, Comanche, Apache, and Sioux.

6 The Tall Chief

Wynkoop believed that Black Kettle had been truthful in his letter, and he made a decision that many thought was foolish and risky. He decided to go to Black Kettle's camp to talk. He asked for volunteers from among his men to go with him. No one stepped forward until One-Eye promised Wynkoop safety to and from the Cheyenne camp.

Wynkoop, 127 volunteers, Chief One-Eye and his party, and an interpreter named John Smith set out at dawn on September 6, 1864. They had with them two **howitzers**, extra horses, tents, ammunition, and a wagon for the hostages. For four days, they rode through buffalo grass, sage, and empty prairie.

On the morning of the fifth day, after traveling around 140 miles, they reached Black Kettle's camp.

Hundreds of Cheyenne warriors armed with rifles, spears, and shields appeared over a ridge. Their faces were covered with red and yellow war paint. Good training and discipline kept Wynkoop's men from fleeing. They tried not to show fear, but they expected to be killed.

Wynkoop ordered his men to prepare for a fight. He sent Chief One-Eye forward to explain to Black Kettle why they had come. After shouting back and forth across open space, the warriors backed off but did not leave. They surrounded the troops and followed until the soldiers made camp. Even then, Wynkoop was not sure he and his men would leave alive.

Know More!

Native American Body Paint

The Plains Indians painted their bodies and their horses to show strength, heroism, and willingness to fight to the death. They also painted their bodies for ceremonies and dances and to simply be admired. Body paints were made from fine clays (dirt) mixed with bear grease or buffalo tallow. Yellow and red were common colors. Yellow paints made with the gall bladder of a buffalo were highly prized. Flowers, tree bark, and other plants were also used to make paints.

Soon after, Wynkoop and three of his officers met with Black Kettle and the main chiefs of the Cheyenne and Arapaho. Wynkoop and his men sat opposite the chiefs in a circle as the peace pipe was passed. Other Indians came to watch. Many of them were unfriendly, and they glared at the white soldiers.

Through interpreters George Bent and John Smith, Wynkoop told the Cheyenne why he had come. He explained about getting the letter and said he came in peace. He asked that the white captives be returned.

The chiefs and other Indians argued loudly among themselves. Why had Wynkoop brought "the guns on wagons" (howitzers) if he came in peace? Bull Bear, a chief of the **Dog Soldiers**, sprang up. He walked toward Wynkoop and demanded that he stand. Then, pointing angrily at Wynkoop, he said his people had traded many horses for the captives. The white man offered them nothing in return. Did Wynkoop think they were fools? Did the soldiers come to laugh at them?

Wynkoop later wrote that the Indians were like "snarling wolves." Everywhere he looked, threatening faces stared back at him. John Smith told Wynkoop that he had better start talking for his life. In the middle of this anger, One-Eye stepped forward. He told the others that he had promised Wynkoop his safety. Wynkoop had come in good faith, and One-Eye had given him the word of a Cheyenne. One-Eye offered Bull Bear two of his own horses to keep the Dog Soldiers from attacking.

Other chiefs spoke. Many thought that the white soldiers should be killed. Finally Chief Black Kettle had his say. In Wynkoop's words, "He arose gathered his robes around him, advanced to where I stood and took me by the hand." He led Wynkoop to the center of the circle and stood next to him. Black Kettle said he believed the "Tall Chief" spoke the truth. Wynkoop had not come with a "forked tongue or with two hearts." He had shown bravery and trust to come to their camp to talk. Black Kettle knew that Wynkoop could not promise peace in exchange for the prisoners. It was only the white chief far away, the Great Father in Washington, DC, who could do this.

Wynkoop watched the chiefs as they listened to Black Kettle. Their eyes no longer flashed with anger. He began to relax. Black Kettle told Wynkoop that he could not speak for the other chiefs. His people would meet that night and decide what to do. Either way, he promised Wynkoop a safe return to Fort Lyon. He

COLONEL EDWARD WYNKOOP AND HIS INTERPRETER.—[SKETCHED BY T. R. DAVIS.]

Colonel Edward Wynkoop and his interpreter as sketched by Theodore Davis in Harper's Weekly magazine, May 11, 1867.

told Wynkoop to ride until the "sun kisses the prairie," make camp, and wait for the Cheyennes' answer.

The next two days were long for Wynkoop, and his nights were sleepless. The soldiers with him insisted they go back to Fort Lyon immediately and not wait for word from the Cheyenne. They were so afraid and angry that Wynkoop feared they would **mutiny**.

Wynkoop's trust in Black Kettle paid off. The Cheyenne returned four captives. The youngest one, golden-haired Isabelle, was only three years old. When she was delivered to Wynkoop, she hugged him and asked for her mama. The men cheered when Wynkoop rode into camp with Isabelle on his saddle. Even the men who had wanted to mutiny celebrated. A few tears slid down the cheeks of the "battle scarred rough soldier[s]."

The celebrating was not finished. Black Kettle and other leaders of the Cheyenne and Arapaho agreed to go with Wynkoop to Denver for a peace talk with Governor Evans. They arrived in Denver on September 28, 1864. From there they rode to Camp Weld, where they met with Colonel Chivington and the governor.

Black Kettle gave a speech. He told the people at Camp Weld that he had come to make peace. He did not want his people to be mistaken as enemies. He and the other chiefs would work to get their people to stop fighting the settlers. This was the best Black Kettle could do. He was a strong voice among the Cheyenne, but there were many other chiefs. It was not the Cheyenne way to tell others what to do. First and foremost, Black Kettle wanted to protect his family and followers.

Wynkoop and the Indians left Camp Weld satisfied that an agreement had been reached. The friendly Cheyenne and Arapaho would gather near Fort Lyon

Major Wynkoop watched from horseback as the Cheyenne and Arapaho arrived in Denver for the Camp Weld Council.

34 Edward Wynkoop

Edward Wynkoop is kneeling on the left. Silas Soule is to his right. Directly behind Wynkoop is Chief Black Kettle. The photograph was taken at the Camp Weld Council where Black Kettle tried to convince Governor Evans that he and other chiefs wanted peace with the white settlers.

under the protection of the military. The Indians did not know that Evans and Chivington had not told them the full truth. Many people in Colorado Territory wanted war with the Indians. They thought all Indians were bad and did not care if they were friendly or not.

7 Bloody Sand Creek

In October the Cheyenne and Arapaho moved and camped near Fort Lyon. Wynkoop gave them food, ammunition for hunting, and other supplies. He waited for instructions on what to do next. The news he received was not what he expected. Major Scott Anthony rode into Fort Lyon with papers that dismissed Wynkoop from his duties. Wynkoop was ordered to report to Fort Riley in north-central Kansas to explain why he had given food and supplies to the Indians without orders to do so.

Wynkoop could not stay at Fort Lyon. If he did, he would be punished for disobeying orders. The officers who had ridden with him to Black Kettle's camp agreed that Wynkoop had done the right thing by freeing the captives from the Dog Soldiers. They also agreed that it had been a good idea to take the chiefs to Camp Weld for peace talks. Since the talks, Indian attacks along the Platte River and throughout Colorado Territory had decreased.

Before Wynkoop left Fort Lyon, he tried to make sure the Indians would be treated with respect. He told Major Anthony that the Arapaho and Cheyenne wanted peace. Wynkoop and Anthony decided the Indians at Fort Lyon should move to Big Sandy Creek where they could remain under the protection of the officers at Fort Lyon.

Wyncoop's officers were sorry to see him go. Lieutenant Joseph Cramer wrote a letter of support for him. It was signed by seven other officers. One of them was Captain Silas Soule. Captain Soule and Lieutenant Cramer had been to Black Kettle's camp with Wynkoop. They believed that Black Kettle and the other chiefs who had been to Camp Weld were honest about working for peace.

As soon as Wynkoop left Fort Lyon, Major Anthony stopped following Wynkoop's **policies**. He arrested Indians who came into the fort for supplies. He also asked the Indians to give up their guns. The Indians did not argue. Chief Left Hand of the Arapaho told

Anthony that he would not fight, even if the soldiers tried to kill him.

Four days after Wynkoop left the fort, one of the worst massacres in Colorado's history occurred. It happened at Sand Creek where the Cheyenne and Arapaho thought they were safe. At dawn on November 29, 1864, soldiers led by Colonel Chivington circled the Indian camp and attacked. Most of the Cheyenne warriors were away from the camp, and the old people, women, and children in the camp were defenseless. Chivington did not hold back his men when women and children ran from their tepees. The soldiers aimed the howitzers and fired.

Chief Black Kettle was in the camp and, at first, tried to calm his people. He told them not to run from the soldiers and that they were at peace with the soldiers. As the bullets ripped through the freezing air, the Cheyenne and Arapaho soon realized the soldiers were there to kill them. Many women and children died in the attack.

The attack lasted throughout the morning. Some of the Indians fought back, and small skirmishes continued throughout the afternoon. Others dug holes in the sandy banks of the creek and hid until after dark. From there, they escaped without blankets or extra clothes. They walked all night in below-freezing weather toward a Dog Soldier camp fifty miles away on the Smoky Hill River. Black Kettle survived. After he found his wounded wife, they joined the march. The survivors tried to make a camp, but they could not overcome the cold. They had to keep moving or freeze to death.

Not all of the soldiers wanted to kill the Indians. Lieutenant Cramer and Captain Soule did not fight. They ordered soldiers under their command to hold

In 1936 Robert Lindeaux painted The Sand Creek Massacre. His painting showed the Arapaho and Cheyenne encampment on November 29, 1864, at the moment of attack. Before his death in 1970, Lindeaux donated the painting to the History Colorado Center.

their fire. Cramer and Soule were later called cowards and scorned for not joining the fight.

The massacre at Sand Creek changed Black Kettle's life. He lost the trust of his people. Before the attack, his people believed him when he said it was possible to make peace with the whites. Afterwards the warriors' voices cried more loudly. Cries for revenge went out to all the other Cheyenne, Arapaho, and Dog Soldier camps. The peace that Black Kettle and Wynkoop had worked for exploded into rage. Attacks, raids, and looting by Indians erupted along the Platte and Arkansas Rivers.

8 Wynkoop Speaks Out

Wynkoop did not hear about the Sand Creek attack until he reached Fort Riley in early December. The details of the massacre came to him in letters from people like Soule and Cramer. He also read in newspapers that Chivington claimed he had killed more than 400 Indians. Wynkoop wondered if Black Kettle and his other Cheyenne friends were alive.

Many people in Colorado wanted to hide the fact that friendly Indians had been attacked at Sand Creek. They wanted to believe that Chivington was a hero and to celebrate his victory over the "savages." Wynkoop had a different view of what happened. He knew the Indians had been killed for no reason, but few people wanted to hear his side of the story. Wynkoop asked for a meeting with General Samuel Curtis, the military commander for Kansas and the West, to explain what he thought had happened on November 29.

Wynkoop was not sure General Curtis would listen. After he presented his evidence and told what he knew, Curtis agreed with him that innocent Indians had been killed by Chivington's men. Instead of punishing Wynkoop, Curtis once again put him in charge of Fort Lyon.

In January 1865, Wynkoop began investigating the massacre. He interviewed soldiers and went to Sand Creek to see the site for himself. The bodies were still where they had fallen. Wynkoop estimated that three-quarters of them were women and children, many of them infants.

Wynkoop continued to speak out against the killings. Three investigations of the Sand Creek Massacre followed. One of them was conducted by the military, and two others were done by special committees from Washington, DC. The Washington investigations noted that officers and soldiers at Sand Creek acted disgracefully and that the attack was unnecessary. A separate report stated the men under Chivington's command "surprised and murdered, in cold blood, the unsuspecting men, women, and children on Sand Creek, who had every reason to believe they were under the protection of the United States authorities."

Most people in the eastern United States agreed with Wynkoop that the killings were wrong. People in Colorado, however, disliked Wynkoop because of his views on Sand Creek. The *Rocky Mountain News* called him an "Indian lover." The paper argued against everything Wynkoop said or did.

> **Know More!**
>
> **Settlers and Indians**
>
> Imagine yourself a settler in Colorado Territory. You have come from another part of the United States or a foreign country to start a new life, but you have heard stories about Indian attacks, stolen livestock, and kidnappings. What do you think your attitude toward Native Americans would be? Do you think that you could have been friends with the Native Americans? What would have prevented or encouraged friendship? What protection would you expect from the territorial and US governments?

9 Working for Peace

Wynkoop had a tough job ahead of him as the commander of Fort Lyon. Following the Sand Creek Massacre, the Southern Cheyenne Indians and the Dog Soldiers increased their attacks on the white settlements. The raiding and looting were worse than they had ever been. Even though he supported Black Kettle and his people, Wynkoop still needed to protect Fort Lyon and the settlers in the area against an attack.

During the spring of 1865, Wynkoop made more improvements to the fort. On March 13, he received an honorary promotion to lieutenant colonel. In June, he was named chief of the cavalry and assigned to Fort Riley. Louise and the children joined him there.

In the fall, Wynkoop was asked to be a part of the peace talks with the Cheyenne and Arapaho at the Little

Arkansas River in Kansas. Many great men gathered for the meeting. They included Indian fighter Kit Carson, and appointed peace **commissioners**: William Bent of Bent's Fort, Colonel William Harney, and General John Sandborn. More than four thousand Cheyenne, Arapaho, Kiowa, Comanche, and Apache were at the peace talks. Though not all of the chiefs attended, Black Kettle was there.

During the peace talks, Wynkoop rode into Black Kettle's camp. It was the first time he had seen the chief since the Sand Creek Massacre, and he was not sure he would be welcome. Black Kettle greeted him in friendship. He told Wynkoop he had not lost faith in him and still believed the Tall Chief spoke the truth. Not everyone was happy to see him though. Remembering Sand Creek, some of the Indian women wailed with grief.

At the end of the talks, the Indians signed the new treaty. The treaty had to be approved by the US Congress. In Washington the treaty was changed to make it less favorable to the Indians. The federal government did not understand the ties the Indians had to their homelands. The Arapaho and Cheyenne did not want to leave the places where the spirits of their ancestors rested. Government officials also did not understand why all the chiefs did not attend the peace talks.

Wynkoop's job was to explain the treaty changes to the Cheyenne and Dog Soldier chiefs and persuade them to sign it. First he would have to find them. The chiefs were difficult to locate because of the distances that separated the bands of Indians and how often they moved. A meeting was set for February 1866 at Bluff Creek in south-central Kansas. Wynkoop sent riders to tell as many chiefs as possible about the meeting and try to get them to come.

Another problem between the US government and the Indians was with the annuities that were promised. They had not been delivered. The winter of 1865 had been cold, and food was scarce. The delay of the food and other items upset the Indians. Wynkoop gathered supplies and brought them to the Bluff Creek meeting. This did little to improve the bad feelings, and Wynkoop feared for his life.

The Dog Soldier chiefs were still hostile toward whites. Each time the US government broke a promise, they grew angrier. Wynkoop convinced the chiefs at the meeting to put their mark on the treaty to indicate that they agreed to the terms. Many Cheyenne did not want to give up their land. After more talks, the Indians at Bluff Creek agreed to sign and move south of the Arkansas River, which was one of the terms of the treaty.

Wynkoop thought he had helped to make travel across the Plains safe again for the settlers. Keeping peace with the Plains Indians depended on the US government keeping the promises made in the treaty.

> ## Know More!
>
> **Understanding Annuities**
>
> Government annuities were part of treaty agreements with the Indians. Because the treaties limited the places the Plains Indians could hunt for buffalo, the government promised them food and other supplies. Annuities included bacon, flour, coffee, sugar, fresh beef, tobacco, clothing, beads, blankets, metal tools, cooking utensils, gunpowder, and bullets. How many of the annuity items had the Indians depended on the buffalo to supply?
>
> With a partner, list the things you would need to survive in the mountains for a week. How much of each item would you need for yourself and others? Compare your list to the list of annuities the Indians were promised. Hint: Wynkoop estimated that the Cheyenne and Arapaho would need 81,000 pounds of flour and 27,000 pounds of bacon each month.

If the annuities were not delivered on time, the peace would not last. For a while, things were better, then Dog Soldiers attacked settlements in Kansas and the tensions on the Plains returned. Wynkoop's superiors thought he had failed. Wynkoop decided it was time to leave military service. In July 1866, he resigned.

10 Indian Agent

Wynkoop still hoped to find a way to help the Indians. Two weeks after he left the military, Wynkoop met with the Commissioner of Indian Affairs in Washington. He told the commissioner that the Cheyenne and Arapaho were not receiving the supplies promised to them in the treaties. Wynkoop was given a new job—to make sure the Indians got the food and annuities they were promised. Later he was named **Indian agent** for the Upper Arkansas Agency.

Wynkoop's job was not easy. If there were any attacks by Indians, Wynkoop was ordered to withhold supplies. It was often hard to know which **band** of Indians was responsible. Wynkoop feared what might happen if they did not get what was promised to them. For the Indians, the annuities meant survival. Without them, they would starve. He also knew that only a few of the Dog Soldiers were responsible for the trouble. When Wynkoop asked for help and more supplies, they did not come.

Another change was happening in the West. The Civil War ended in 1865, and many of the officers of that war were sent west to command western forts. Kansas had become a state in 1861, and Nebraska would soon follow. Settlers continued to **migrate** to areas along the Platte River and into Colorado Territory. They needed military protection, but the new officers did not understand the Indians or the Indian ways. Instead of trying to talk with the Indians to solve the problems, they wanted to act with full force.

Wynkoop arranged meetings between the Indians and the officers, but the officers made threats and did not listen. The Indians wanted to ride to the forts to get supplies without being threatened or shot. The military officers banned them from coming into the forts. The Indians were also afraid of the soldiers coming close to their own camps. In the past, their villages had been burned and looted by the military.

On one occasion, Civil War hero General Winfield Scott Hancock insisted on a meeting with the Cheyenne at their camp. Tall Bull, speaking for his people, asked Wynkoop to stop Hancock. The Cheyenne were afraid they would be attacked like Black Kettle's people at Sand Creek. Wynkoop tried to reason with Hancock, but Hancock pushed forward. As Hancock neared the camp, he learned that most of the Indians had run away.

This angered Hancock. He ordered Lieutenant Colonel George Armstrong Custer to surround the camp. When Custer's soldiers arrived, only a few Cheyenne remained. Custer tried to follow the fleeing Indians but was unable to track them. As he traveled, he came across the burned-out ruins and **mutilated** bodies of whites at Lookout Station, a stage stop along the Smoky Hill Trail in Kansas. He thought the killings had been done by the Cheyenne and sent word to Hancock. In anger Hancock ordered Tall Bear's camp to be burned. In the end, it was not the Cheyenne who were responsible for the killings at the stage stop.

Wynkoop thought the whole matter could have been avoided. He wrote letters of protest, but they arrived too late to help. Wynkoop believed that the peaceful and innocent Indians had suffered for the actions of a few **renegades**. He continued to speak out but was criticized by whites and Indians alike. He was blamed by both sides for the burning of the Cheyenne camp. This did not stop Wynkoop from working to bring the two sides together.

In October 1867, another peace council was held at Medicine Lodge Creek west of Fort Larned in Kansas. The Kiowa, Comanche, Arapaho, Plains Apache, and Southern Cheyenne attended. Although many Cheyenne were angry with Wynkoop, he was still considered one of the few white men who could be trusted. As with the other meetings, Wynkoop walked a rocky path between the two cultures. He worked hard to find a peaceful agreement, and the Plains Indians signed a treaty. Once again, however, many of the terms were changed in Washington.

The Cheyenne and Arapaho believed they could now hunt buffalo as far north as the Platte River. This was a misunderstanding. The 1867 treaty stated they could only hunt south of the Arkansas River. As long as the buffalo stayed south of the Arkansas, this worked fine. The Indians depended on the buffalo for food. When the buffalo migrated north of the Arkansas, they had nothing to eat. Wynkoop did not sign the treaty.

Wynkoop once again fought to have supplies provided for the Indians. He delivered them as quickly as he could. The shipments came from the East. Supplies were sometimes delivered to the wrong place, lost, or even sold by dishonest agents for a profit. This made Wynkoop's job harder.

Communication on the Plains was slow. When the annuities were delivered to the wrong place it took days to fix the problem. This angered the Indians and made them more mistrusting of the whites. Poor communication also affected some of the actions of the military. Rumors flew and often the wrong Indians were blamed. The military took action before any official word came. If mail was delayed or the telegraph lines damaged, messages took even longer.

As hard as he tried, Wynkoop could not prevent Indian raids. Wynkoop explained to the military that the warriors did not represent all Indians. He tried to keep the peaceful Indians safe. The angry young warriors continued to attack. Instead of getting better, life on the Plains became more unsettled and dangerous. General William Tecumseh Sherman, the head of the district, wanted to settle the Indian problem "one way of the other." He gave orders to "treat friendly bands with kindness" but "show no mercy" to the others. His officers, however, did not distinguish between the peaceful Indians and the warring Indians.

On November 27, 1868, the cavalry under the command of Lieutenant Colonel Custer attacked Black Kettle's camp along the Washita River. The attack was very similar to the one at Sand Creek four years earlier.

This time Black Kettle and his wife were killed. As at Sand Creek, many women and children died, but the reports did not agree on how many.

When Wynkoop learned of Black Kettle's death, he wrote a letter of resignation. In the letter he said he could no longer watch the murder of Indians. He still believed there were ways to solve the problems peacefully. He returned to the East. When he reached Washington, DC, Wynkoop talked to anyone who would listen about the struggles of the Plains Indians. He was asked how he thought the problem should be solved. He answered that the Indians should become full citizens and have seats in Congress.

Wynkoop hoped to get another job that would allow him to help the Indians. When Ulysses S. Grant became president in March 1869, his hope faded. Grant wanted to make changes. This included using new people for jobs in the West. With his new policy, Grant offered peace to the Indians, but at the same time, the military took a firm stand. They pushed the Indians to **reservations** and kept them there. No more treaties were made.

11 Wynkoop's Lasting Legacy

In the fall of 1869, Wynkoop went into business with his brother John in Pennsylvania. They operated a large furnace used to make pig iron, a type of iron used in steel. As with other things, Wynkoop learned the job quickly and the business began to show a profit.

Wynkoop did not return to the West until 1875, when gold was discovered in Deadwood, Dakota Territory. He was in poor health, and because of an earlier injury, it was painful for him to ride a horse. He returned to his family in Pennsylvania in June 1876.

Wynkoop moved west one last time. In his new job as a special US timber agent, he was responsible for protecting forests on government-owned land. He moved his family to Sante Fe, New Mexico. He and Louise now had eight children. After that job ended,

Wynkoop oversaw the Voluntary Militia of the Territory of New Mexico. His last job was working as a prison **warden** in New Mexico Territory. Always a man of action, Wynkoop set to work to make improvements in prison life. He built a hospital for the inmates and started a four-acre garden that provided vegetables for the inmates year round.

Edward W. Wynkoop died September 11, 1891. The *Santa Fe Daily New Mexican* newspaper called him "honest, big hearted," and "as true as steel."

Much had changed during his fifty-five years of life. When he was born, what we now know as the state of Colorado did not exist. The Indians roamed freely, following the buffalo herds and living according to their own traditions. Few white people lived west of the Mississippi River.

By 1860 as many as 5,000 wagons a year traveled the Santa Fe Trail to reach the far west. The arrival of the whites threatened the survival of the Native Americans of the Plains. By 1869 the Transcontinental Railroad was completed, connecting the east to the west. By 1890 the population of Denver, the town Wynkoop had helped found, had grown to more than 100,000. Life on the Plains had changed forever. The large buffalo herds vanished, and the days of when Native Americans followed the herds over the vast prairie landscape became a memory.

Very few people who came west to settle called the native americans their friends. Most white Americans thought of them as backward savages. Lieutenant Colonel Edward Wynkoop was different. He took a risk and crossed the barrier between the cultures. He wanted to find a way for the whites and Indians to live together in peace. He continued to speak for the Indians of the Plains for as long as he lived.

Timeline

1821 — Santa Fe Trail opened.

1834 — Bent's Fort was completed.

1836 — Edward Wynkoop was born in Philadelphia, Pennsylvania.

1856 — Edward traveled west to join his sister and brother-in-law in Lecompton, Kansas Territory.

1858 — Gold was discovered in western Kansas Territory where the mouth of Little Dry Creek met the South Platte. This started the Pikes Peak Gold Rush—later named the Colorado Gold Rush.

1858 — Wynkoop joined a land development company heading for Arapahoe County in western Kansas Territory.

1859 — Wynkoop became one of the founders of Denver when he returned to Kansas to file papers to set up the new town.

1859 — In the fall, Wynkoop returned to Denver City to start his new life as sheriff of Arapahoe County.

1860 — Abraham Lincoln was elected president.

1861 — Colorado became a territory, and William Gilpin was appointed territorial governor.

1861 — The first shots of the Civil War were fired at Fort Sumter, South Carolina.

1861 — Governor Gilpin organized two companies of volunteers to protect Colorado Territory from a Confederate invasion.

1861 — July 31, Wynkoop enlisted as a Colorado Volunteer.

1862 — In March, Wynkoop and other Colorado Volunteers defeated the Confederates in the Battle of Glorietta Pass in New Mexico.

1862 — After the Battle of Glorietta Pass, Wynkoop was promoted to major and stationed at Fort Craig.

1863 — Wynkoop returned to Camp Weld near Denver City.

1863 – 1864 — Tensions between the settlers and the Indians of the Plains grew.

1864 — In May, Wynkoop was assigned to the command of Fort Lyon in southeastern Colorado.

1864 — Lieutenant Eayre attacked a group of Cheyenne camped near Ash Creek and killed two Indian chiefs.

1864 — June 27, Governor John Evans wrote a letter, "To the Friendly Indians of the Plains" telling them to go to the nearest fort for protection.

1864 — In September, Wynkoop traveled with Chief One-Eye to Black Kettle's camp to discuss peace and the release of white captives.

1864 — September 28, Chief Black Kettle and other Indian representatives arrive in Camp Weld near Denver for a peace council with Governor Evans and Colonel John Chivington.

1864 — In October, Chief Black Kettle and Chief Left Hand moved their camps near Fort Lyon for protection.

1864 — On November 5, Wynkoop was relieved of his duties at Fort Lyon by Major Scott Anthony.

1864 — In mid-November, Cheyenne and Arapaho Indians moved their camps to Sandy Creek.

1864 — November 26, Wynkoop left Fort Lyon as ordered to report to Fort Riley.

1864 — November 29, Colorado Volunteers and Calvalry attacked and murdered the Indians camped at Sandy Creek. What is now known as the Sand Creek Massacre started at dawn and continued throughout the day.

1865 — Early January, Wynkoop returned to the command of Fort Lyon to investigate what happened at Sand Creek.

1865 — February 11, the military investigation of Sand Creek began by the Joint Committee on the Conduct of War.

1865 — March 13, Wynkoop received the honorary rank of Lieutenant Colonel.

1865 — April 9, the Civil War ended when General Robert E. Lee surrendered in Virginia.

1865 — In October, Wynkoop attended the peace talks for the Little Arkansas Treaty.

1866 — Wynkoop resigned from military service.

1868 — November 27, Black Kettle and his wife were killed at the Battle of Washita in Oklahoma Territory.

1868 — November 29, Wynkoop resigned his job as Indian agent.

1869 — Wynkoop returned to Pennyslvania and went into business with his brother.

1875 — Wynkoop moved to Dakota Territory for a year.

1876 — Colorado became a state.

1882 — Wynkoop and his family moved to Santa Fe, New Mexico. Wynkoop took a job as a US timber agent.

1890 — Wynkoop worked as a warden for the New Mexico prisons.

1891 — September 11, Edward Wynkoop died in Santa Fe.

Glossary

Abolitionist: a person who is in favor of abolishing slavery.

Band: a group of Indians who share culture and territory and are self-governing.

Boomtown: a town experiencing a sudden growth in population.

Buckskins: clothing made from soft, flexible leather made from deer hide.

Commissioners: persons who have authority to act as agent for another person or group.

Dog Soldiers: a Cheyenne warrior society.

Frontier: a region at the edge of the settled part of a country.

Frostbite: condition of having the surface tissues of some part of the body frozen.

Homesteaders: settlers in a new area who work to own US public land by living on and farming the land for a few years.

Howitzers: short cannons capable of firing a shell in a high arc.

Incorporate: to form, make into, or become a corporation.

Indian agent: an individual who interacts with Native American tribes as a representative of the US government.

Interpreters: persons who translate for people speaking different languages.

Mesa: a flat-topped hill or small plateau with steep sides.

Migrate: to move from one country, place, or locality to another.

Militia: a group of citizens with some military training who are called to active duty only in an emergency.

Mutilated: caused severe damage to the body of a person or animal.

Mutiny: a situation in which a group of people refuse to obey orders and try to take control away from the person who commands them.

Plains Indians: the tribes of American Indians who lived a nomadic life following the buffalo in the Great Plains of North America.

Policies: actions agreed upon to guide and determine present and future decisions.

Population: the number of people living in a country or region.

Proclamation: a formal public announcement.

Rations: a food allowance for one day.

Reinforcements: additional personnel or materials.

Renegades: persons who leave one group and join an opposing group.

Reservations: areas of land in the US that are kept separate as a place for Native Americans to live.

Retaliated: sought revenge.

Ruffians: violent persons who threaten and hurt other people.

Seceded: separated from a nation or state and became independent.

Skirmish: a minor fight between small groups of troops.

Slavery: the practice of owning another person.

Surveyor: someone whose job is to find out the size, shape, and position of an area of land.

Truce: a temporary stop in fighting.

Warden: an official in charge of a prison.

Bibliography

Bacon, Melvin and Blegen, Daniel. *Bent's Fort: Crossroads of Cultures on the Santa Fe Trail*. Palmer Lake, Colo. Filter Press, LLC, 2002.

Bailey A. "March 17, 1863, Lincoln Meets with the Indians." Sevencoreandtenyears.com. *http://www.7score10years.com/index. php/north/82-north/1019-march-27-1863-lincoln-meets-with-indians* (accessed January 10, 2014).

Bennett, W. Charles, Jr. (editor) *"Reminiscences of Edward W. Wynkoop* 1856-1858." Emporia.edu *https://esirc.emporia.edu/bitstream/ handle/123456789/714/BennettJr%20Vol%2011%20Num%203. pdf?sequence=1* (accessed January 10, 2014)

Berthrong, Donald J. *The Southern Cheyennes*. Norman: University of Oklahoma Press, 1963.

Civil War Trust. "Glorietta Pass." Civilwar.org. *http://www.civilwar.org/ battlefields/glorieta-pass.html?tab=facts* (accessed January 10, 2014).

Civil War Trust. "Maps of Glorieta Pass, New Mexico (1862) Battle of Glorieta Pass — The Fight for Pigeon's Ranch, March 28, 1862." Civilwar.org *http://www.civilwar.org/battlefields/glorietapass/maps/ glorietapassmap.html* (accessed January 10, 2014).

Gerboth, Christopher B., ed. *The Tall Chief: The Autobiography of Edward W. Wynkoop*. Denver: Colorado Historical Society, 1994.

Greene, Jerome A., and Douglas D. Scott. *Finding Sand Creek*. Norman: University of Oklahoma Press, 2004.

Fort Hays State University. "Homesteading in Ellis County: Fort Hays." Fhsu.edu. *http://www.fhsu.edu/library/ksheritage/Fort-Hays/* (accessed January 10, 2014).

Halaas, David F., and Andrew E. Masich. *Halfbreed*. Cambridge, Mass.: Da Capo Press, 2004.

Hatch, Thom. *Black Kettle*. Hoboken, N.J.: John Wiley & Sons, Inc., 2004.

Hoig, Stan. *The Sand Creek Massacre.* Norman: University of Oklahoma Press, 1961.

Kansapedia, Kansas Historical Society. "Medicine Lodge Peace Treaty." Kshs.org. *http://www.kshs.org/kansapedia/medicine-lodge-peace-treaty/16709* (accessed January 10, 2014).

Kansas Geneaology. "Bent's Fort, Kansas History." Kansas Geneology.com *http://www.kansasgenealogy.com/history/bents_fort.htm* (accessed January 10, 2014).

KC Lonewolf. "Edward W. Wynkoop." Kclonewolf.com. *http://www.kclonewolf.com/History/SandCreek/Bio/edward-wynkoop-biography.html* (accessed January 10, 2014).

KC Lonewolf. "Sand Creek Massacre, Weld Council Transcript." Kclonewolf.com. *http://www.kclonewolf.com/History/SandCreek/sc-documents/sc-weld-council.html* (accessed January 10, 2014). (This page includes a summary followed by the translated transcript of the Weld Council and a letter written by Governor John Evans, following the meeting.)

KC Lonewolf. "The Sand Creek Massacre." Kclonewolf.com. *http://www.kclonewolf.com/History/SandCreek/sc-index.html* (accessed January 10, 2014). (This page is a summary with links to documents and a multitude of resources about the Massacre.)

KC Lonewolf. "The Sand Creek Massacre, Major Edward Wynkoop Reports on Smoky Hill Council." Kclonewolf.com. *http://www.kclonewolf.com/History/SandCreek/sc-reports/report-wynkoop-smoky-hill.html* (accessed January 10, 2014).

Kraft, Louis. *Ned Wynkoop and the Lonely Road from Sand Creek.* Norman: University of Oklahoma Press, 2011.

National Archives, OPA-Online Public Access "Treaty of Little Arkansas River, October 14, 1865 (Ratified Indian Treaties #341, 14 STAT 703) between the U.S. and Arapahoe and Cheyenne Indians (Black Kettle Band) granting lands in reparation for the Sand Creek Massacre, November 29, 1864., 11/29/1864 - 10/14/1865." Research.archives.gov. *http://research.archives.gov/description/299802* (accessed January 10, 2014)

National Park Service. "Battle of Glorieta Pass." Pecos National Historic Park, New Mexico. *http://www.nps.gov/peco/historyculture/copy-of-battleofglorietta.htm* (accessed January 10, 2014).

National Park Service. "Fort Larned National Historic Site, Larned, Kansas." Nps.gov. *http://www.nps.gov/nr/travel/cultural_diversity/Fort_Larned_National_Historic_Site.html* (accessed January 10, 2014).

Noel, Tom. "Apollo Hall was birthplace of government, theatrical events." http://m.rockymountainnews.com/news/2006/nov/18/bnoel-b-apollo-hall-was-birthplace-of-government/. Published November 18, 2006. (accessed March 24, 2014).

Santa Fe Trail Research Site. "Old Fort Wise-Lyon, Colorado." Santafetrailresearch.com. *http://www.santafetrailresearch.com/spacepix/old-fort-wise-lyon.html* (accessed January 10, 2014).

This Day in History. *"Feb 28, 1861:* Congress creates Colorado Territory." History.com *http://www.history.com/this-day-in-history/congress-creates-colorado-territory* (accessed January 10, 2014).

Visit Denver, the Convention and Visitor's Bureau. "Denver's Beginnings." Denver, the Mile High City. *http://www.denver.org/metro/history* (accessed January 10, 2014).

West Film Project. "John M. Chivington (1821-1894)." Pbs.org. *http://www.pbs.org/weta/thewest/people/a_c/chivington.htm* (accessed January 10, 2014).

West Film Project. "William Tecumseh Sherman" Pbs.org. *http://www.pbs.org/weta/thewest/people/s_z/sherman.htm* (accessed January 10. 2014).

Wynkoop, Christopher H. "Edward Wanshaer Wynkoop" Ancestry.com. *http://freepages.genealogy.rootsweb.ancestry.com/~wynkoop/webdocs/nedwkp.htm* (accessed January 10, 2014). (This site has Wynkoop's life organized chronologically in sections with primary documents referenced and linked in each section.)

Zwink, Timothy A. "E. W. Wynkoop and the Bluff Creek Council, 1866." Kansas Historical Society. *http://www.kshs.org/p/kansas-historical-quarterly-e-w-wynkoop-and-the-bluff-creek-council-1866/13270* (accessed January 10, 2014).

Index

American Civil War, 13, 14–18
Anthony, Major Scott, 35, 36–37
Arapahoe County, Kansas, 5, 21
Arkansas River, 39, 46, 51
Ash Creek, 24, 25

Battle of Glorieta Pass, 16–17, 18
Bent, George, 29
Bent, William, 44
Black Kettle, 1, 25–30, 32–33, 34, 36, 37–38, 39, 43, 44, 52–53
Bluff Creek, Kansas, 45–46
Brindle, Emily and William, 2, 3, 4
Bull Bear, 29, 30

Camp Weld, 15, 16, 18, 22, 32
Camp Weld Council, 33, 34, 36
Carson, Kit, 44
Chivington, John M., 15–17, 21, 24, 25, 26, 32, 34, 37, 40, 41
Cramer, Joseph, 36, 38–39, 40
Curtis, Samuel, 40, 41
Custer, George Armstrong, 50, 52

Dakota Territory, 54
Denver City/Denver, 7, 11–14, 21, 26, 32, 55
Denver City Land Company, 9, 11
Denver, James W., 5, 7
Dog Soldiers, 29, 30, 35, 43, 47, 49

Eayre, George, 22, 24 – 25
Evans, Governor John, 26, 32, 34

Fort Craig, New Mexico, 18
Fort Lyon, Colorado, 23, 24, 25, 26, 30, 32, 34, 35, 36, 41, 43
Fort Riley, Kansas, 35, 40, 43

Gilpin, William, 14
Grant, President Ulysses, 53

Hancock, Winfield Scott, 49–50

Larimer, William, 7
Lean Bear, 24–25
Lecompton, Kansas, 4, 11
Left Hand, 12, 36
Lincoln, President Abraham, 13, 24–25
Lindeaux, Robert, 38

Medicine Lodge Creek, 51

One-Eye, 26, 27, 28, 29–30

Philadelphia, Pennsylvania, 1
Platte River, 25, 36, 49, 51

Rocky Mountain News, 12, 13, 22, 42

Sand Creek Massacre, 35–39, 40–42, 43, 53
Santa Fe, New Mexico, 16, 17, 18, 55
Santa Fe Trail, 55
Sherman, General William T., 52

Sibley, General Henry, 16
Slough, General John, 17
Smith, John, 27, 29
Soule, Silas, 25, 34, 36, 38, 39, 41
St. Charles Town Company, 7, 11
Steinberger, Albert, 10–11
St. Louis, Missouri, 4

Tall Bull, 49

Wakely, Louise, 13, 14, 18, 19, 43, 54
Washita River, 52
Wynkoop, Edward W.
  Arapahoe County sheriff, 5, 12, 13, 14
  birth, 1
  Civil War service, 14–18
  death, 55
  indian agent, 48–53
  marriage, 14, 18
  Sand Creek Massacre, 40–42

Acknowledgments

I would like to acknowledge Louis Kraft, biographer and author of *Ned Wynkoop and the Lonely Road from Sand Creek*. Without his book and his in-depth research and knowledge, my own understanding of Wynkoop's life would have been far less complete. I would also like to thank Doris Baker of Filter Press, LLC, for encouraging me to write a biography for young readers. It has been both a challenge and a delight.

About the Author

Nancy Oswald is an award-winning author, speaker, and retired elementary teacher. She writes middle grade and young adult historical fiction set in Colorado.

Her other Filter Press titles include: *Nothing Here but Stones*, *Hard Face Moon*, *Rescue in Poverty Gulch*, and *Trouble on the Tracks*.

Nancy lives on a working cattle ranch in the Sangre de Cristo Mountains of Colorado. Contact her for presentations, school visits, and signings through her website, http://www.NancyOswald.com or by emailing authors@FilterPressBooks.com

MORE NOW YOU KNOW BIOS

Florence Sabin
1871 – 1953
Teacher, Scientist,
Humanitarian
ISBN 978-0-86541-139-5

John Denver
1943 – 1997
Singer, songwriter, world-known performer, and humanitarian.
ISBN 978-086541-088-6

Dottie Lamm
1937 –
Former first lady of Colorado and social activist.
ISBN 978-086541-085-5

Emily Griffith
1868 – 1947
Educator and founder of Denver's Emily Griffith Opportunity School.
ISBN 978-0-86541-077-0

José Dario Gallegos
1830 – 1883
Founder of San Luis, oldest town in Colorado.
ISBN 978-0-86541-084-8

John Wesley Powell
1834 – 1902
Soldier, Explorer, Scientist. Led the first exploration of the Grand Canyon.
ISBN 978-0-86541-080-0

Justina Ford
1871 – 1952
The first African-American woman to practice medicine in CO.
ISBN 978-0-86541-074-9

Enos Mills
1870 – 1922
The father of Rocky Mountain National Park.
ISBN 978-0-86541-072-5

Martha Maxwell
1831 – 1881
Naturalist, innovative taxidermist, museum builder.
ISBN 978-0-86541-075-6

Molly Brown
1867 – 1932
Heroine of the Titanic and philanthropist.
ISBN 978-0-86541-081-7

General William Palmer
1836 – 1909
Railroad pioneer, founder of Colorado Springs, and Civil War hero.
ISBN 978-0-86541-092-3

Chipeta
1843 – 1924
Ute peacemaker and wife of Chief Ouray.
ISBN 978-0-86541-091-6

Mary Elitch Long
1856 – 1936
Founder of Elitch Gardens Amusement Park in Denver, CO.
ISBN 978-0-86541-094-7

Bob Sakata
1926 –
American farmer and community leader.
ISBN 978-0-86541-093-0

Susan Anderson
1870 – 1960
Pioneer mountain doctor
By Lydia Griffith
ISBN 978-0-86541-108-1

Framk Craig
1877 – 1914
Founded the Brotherly Relief Colony for destitute consumptives, now the Craig Rehabilitation Hospital
ISBN 978-0-86541-029-3

Now You Know Bios are available at your local bookstore, by calling 888.570.2663, and online at www.FilterPressBooks.com

www.ingramcontent.com/pod-product-compliance
Lightning Source LLC
Chambersburg PA
CBHW062104290426
44110CB00022B/2705